CONNIE

Lessons from a life in the saddle

BY DAVID HORSEY

PHOTOGRAPHS BY DAVID HORSEY, SALLY TONKIN & BILL AYERS

ISBN: 978-1482347609

CONTENTS

THANK YOU

Putting this book together has taken 20 months. Some of the poems
and sayings I have written down, some I have thought up myself. My favorite
was from Tom Tescher, a top professional bronc rider in the '50s and '60s, who said,
"I hope I am wise in advice and slow to offer it, unless asked."
I want to thank David Horsey and Evelyn Iritani for taking the time and trouble to put
this book together. Also, for all of you who took the time to send pictures, thank you.

– CONNIE COX

ACKNOWLEDGMENTS

THIS BOOK WOULD HAVE BEEN TWICE AS HARD TO PRODUCE WITHOUT THE AID OF EXCELLENT FRIENDS.

FOREMOST, I WANT TO THANK EVELYN IRITANI WHO HELPED KEEP ME AND THIS PROJECT ON TRACK.

SHE PARTICIPATED IN INTERVIEWS, TOOK THE LEAD WITH MARKETING AND EVEN CONTRIBUTED A FEW PHOTOS.

HUGE THANKS ARE DUE TO SALLY TONKIN AND BILL AYERS FOR ALLOWING ME

TO USE SO MANY OF THEIR FINE PHOTOGRAPHS TO SUPPLEMENT MINE.

PENNY NICHOLLS HELPED ROUND OUT THE STORY, AS DID SEVERAL RODEO VETERANS,

INCLUDING ED SOLOMON, WADE BICKFORD, DICK GRANNELL AND WIN GAUDI.

MY GRATITUDE ALSO GOES TO MY RIDING BUDDY, PHILL BAILY, WHO LET ME PUBLISH HIS POEM,

"ZN RECOLLECTIONS." (I ALSO APPRECIATE HIS FREQUENT LOANS OF A HORSE.)

PLUS, A TIP OF THE HAT TO BILL COFFIN FOR DOING THE RESEARCH TO DEVELOP THE MAP OF THE ZN.

ROGER AINSLEY, A GREAT FRIEND AND A FINE JOURNALIST, HELPED EDIT THE TEXT — THANKS, ROGER.

I WANT TO RECOGNIZE PAUL MASSON, WHO INTRODUCED ME TO THE EPIC TRAILS EXPERIENCE IN THE FIRST PLACE,

AS WELL AS THE ASPIRING COWBOYS AND COWGIRLS WHOSE FACES SHOW UP IN THIS BOOK,

INCLUDING ANNE NOGATCH, DON ANDERSON, ANN GRAHAM, CONNIE LODELL, CINDY AND KATHY SIDARIS,

SALLY WALKER, KATHY AND STEVE DENNIS, LINDA AND JERRY CUFLEY, GREG WEGELER, BOB PRESCOTT,

CLEO AND SARA BUYTAERT, TACIE AND PETE SALTONSTALL, STEVE KRAUS, BETSY KELLER,

ROXANNE HOON ROBINSON, TONI JO WOODRUFF AND MY SON, DANIEL HORSEY.

A BIG THANK YOU GOES TO CLINTON AND DENISE COX

FOR ALLOWING US ALL TO TRAIPSE ACROSS THEIR RANCH EVERY YEAR.

THE SAME GOES FOR LARRY AND RON KINSELLA AND TED SOLOMON, OUR RANCHER HOSTS NEAR HAVRE.

MY WIFE, NOLE ANN ULERY-HORSEY, DESERVES CREDIT FOR GIVING ME THE FREEDOM TO RUN OFF TO MONTANA

WHEN THE URGE STRIKES AND FOR PATIENTLY SEEING ME THROUGH THE LONG HOURS SPENT DESIGNING THIS BOOK.

AND, FINALLY, I WANT TO THANK CONNIE COX FOR ROPING ME INTO THIS PROJECT. HE GAVE ME FREE REIN TO TELL

HIS STORY. HE HAS BECOME A GOOD FRIEND AND I HOPE I HAVE DONE HIM JUSTICE.

– DAVID HORSEY

Any man who can
make a living doing
what he likes is lucky,
and I am that.
I believe in luck
and I have lots of it.
Any time I cash in now,
I win.

As a rancher and
part time rodeo rider,
there's a better
way to make a living,
but no better
way to live.

– Connie Cox,
Havre, Montana. 2012

1 • SADDLE UP

Conrad Cox was 27 years old that September day in 1960 when two horses went to meet their Maker.

Connie had been riding the amateur rodeo circuit since he was 20, so he was a veteran. This was just another rodeo in Chinook, Montana; just one more opening event aboard a bareback bronc, with Connie hoping to stay on top for eight seconds and bring home some prize money.

He was getting keyed up for his first ride when a hard rain and bolts of lightning sent the crowd rushing for cover. A long half hour dragged by before the clouds parted, the sun returned and the spectators climbed out of their pickups and cars and reclaimed their places in the stands. Connie was nervous. That was typical, but the stormy interruption had not made it any easier.

For an hour before any ride, he avoided conversation. In fact, he could not talk. He was consumed with the bottled-up energy of an athlete waiting to perform. When the time finally came to lower himself onto the bare back of the bucking bronc, it was like straddling a hand grenade with the pin about to be pulled. But Connie felt no fear, just focus. He nodded his head to indicate he was ready to go. The gate swung open. The horse exploded out of the chute with Connie holding on, his spurs raking the animal's flanks and one arm reaching to the sky above. The horse jumped, hopped, bucked – and then ran right into a post and crumpled to the dirt. Connie was left clinging to the top fence rail. The bronc was dead, his neck broken.

Connie climbed down from the fence unharmed but bewildered. This sort of thing did not happen every day. Still, he shook it off and walked over to wait with the rest of the cowboys in back of the chutes. He took some ribbing from the other young men, made a couple of jokes, then felt the nervousness build and the quiet set in again. When the saddle bronc competition was announced, Connie climbed the steps to meet his second ride. Easing down into the cramped chute, he settled into the saddle. The bay horse flexed and fumed underneath him.

The gate swung open. The twisting, leaping and kicking began. The horse did its best to throw Connie. He did his best to hold on, leaning way back, raking the sides of the animal with his spurs. And then the horse shot into a corner, smacked into a fence and dropped dead.

Same afternoon, same cowboy, riding two horses that both hit a fence and died. Things like that never happen. But it happened to young Connie Cox.

It's enough to make a man feel philosophical.

*****

All these years later, Connie survives and keeps on going. He ambles through a corral with the gait of a sailor who has just hit dry land after months at sea. His body has been battered by years of rough rides, not just in his rodeo days, but in days more recent when a young horse decided to dump the old cowboy in the dirt. Yet, when he lurches back into the saddle and rides out to tend another herd, the decades and the aches and the pains fade away. The horse's legs become his own and Connie is that 27-year-old rodeo cowboy again.

There are lessons to be learned from men like Connie Cox. And I have to say, there are many such men in the rangelands of Montana and elsewhere in the West; men who have worked hard most days of their lives and who will not be retiring to ride a golf cart and chase a little white ball around some unnatural expanse of perfectly manicured country club grass. No, these men will still be riding a horse under a big sky, moving skittering cows until the day they die – or close to it.

However, though Connie is, in many ways, typical of the ranchers and cowboys of the American West, he is also a unique character. In a gathering of city folk, many of his peers would naturally set themselves apart, feeling that odd yin and yang of inferiority and superiority that seems common among country people. The sense of inferiority comes from thinking maybe they cannot match the education or worldliness of the city folk; the feeling of superiority comes from knowing these people who spend their lives caught in freeway traffic and captured in office cubicles have no idea how to ride a horse at a gallop while twirling the loop of a rope and aiming it at the head or heels of a running calf. Or how to mend a fence in the broiling summer sun or help a mama cow give birth in the middle of a killer blizzard. Or any of the other hard-earned skills it takes to run a ranch.

If Connie has these mixed feelings, he doesn't show them much. He likes people – even if they are from Seattle or New York or Brussels. He wants to know their stories and he is happy to show them his way of life. Many cowboys are quiet. Connie likes a conversation – although his way of talking is elliptical. He starts with one subject,

2

chases another thought in a different direction, throws in a passage of well-rehearsed wit, leaves a few sentences dangling and finally loops back to where he began. I do not know if he has always talked this way. Perhaps his failing ears contribute to the style (if he cannot quite hear what you're asking, he'll give an answer to what he thinks you said, which is usually just as interesting). Connie is very much a man of his place, the ranchlands of northeast Montana, yet he is curious about the world and, especially, the people who come from that world to learn from him.

Connie tells a well-worn joke about his limited education, saying he was kept in third grade until he was 16, then kicked out because the teacher started bringing apples to *him*. However incomplete his formal education may have actually been, he has learned a great deal in the school of life. Connie is a philosopher in his own way, a collector of profundities and witticisms that he memorizes and employs as borrowed eloquence. These are not just conversational props; they are ideas that matter to him. He may be unable to fully articulate his own philosophy, but taken together, the sayings he rattles off around the campfire or out on a ride looking for stray cattle, add up to real wisdom.

At this point in his life, Connie wanted to finally gather together some of his thoughts, stories and observations and he drafted me to get them down on paper. In two formal interviews and many passing conversations, he talked about his life in the saddle. Piecing it together in a coherent fashion is an interesting task; a little like rousting a cluster of sneaky cows out of a thicket. The best approach is not necessarily straight ahead. A slow meander toward the subject may be the smartest way to go.

So, let's saddle up and start the meander into the life and mind of Conrad Cox.

I WOULD
RATHER
YOU WATCH
AND DO
THAN FOR
ME TO
INSTRUCT
AND TELL.

I WOULD
RATHER
BE ALL RIGHT
HALF THE
TIME THAN
HALF RIGHT
ALL THE
TIME.

~ CONNIE COX

2 • "THIS IS LIVIN'"

The first time I saw Connie, he was stretched out on a bed in a guest room at the Edgewater Motel in Malta, Montana.

A fellow I'd met at the Ellensburg Rodeo had told me the closest I might ever get to real cowboying would be to partake in a roundup with an old rancher named Connie Cox. This sounded good to me. A complete city boy, I'd come to my love of horses and cow herding late in life, inspired by a few days of riding in Los Angeles, of all places. I had stayed a couple of times at a guest ranch in Western Montana, a place where they took horsemanship seriously, fed me well, housed me in a log cabin that looked as if it were furnished by Ralph Lauren and expected a rather large fee in return for their services. I had also ridden with some real cowboys for a couple of days on a big ranch near White Sulphur Springs. It had been just enough to make me eager for the real thing if I could find a place relaxed enough to trust me with a horse and a herd.

So, after a two-day drive from Seattle, I arrived in Malta, the rendezvous point for a small group of novices who were eager to play cowboy. I found the motel and was directed to a corner room where Connie was taking a nap. I knocked on the door and a voice from inside told me to come on in.

There was Connie, lying on the bed in his stocking feet, jeans and plaid shirt. He hopped up to meet me – well, maybe it wasn't a hop; more of a slow launch. He gave me a crooked smile, a solid handshake and words of welcome in a high, husky Western twang. Connie told me this year's crew would be gathering shortly at a steak place in town where we would get acquainted and go over the plan for the week.

That 10-person team consisted mostly of paying guests like me – a bunch I would come to call the Seattle Cowboys, though three hailed from California. We were paying Connie and his business partner, Penny Nicholls, for food and the loan of a horse, if we hadn't brought our own, and for whatever guidance we needed on our path as apprentice cowboys. Beyond that, as I would learn, this would be nothing like any guest ranch I'd ever experienced or heard about.

After trading our personal histories over Montana beef and baked potatoes, Connie led us all down the street to the VFW hall where a country dance was in full swing. For a guy who grew up in Seattle, the scene was as exotic as a market in Morocco. A full bar offering cheap drinks stood at the front of the low-ceilinged hall; at the back was a stage overflowing with multiple guitarists, fiddle players, banjo pickers, a guy on keyboards and a drummer or two. In between, hunched at tables or two-stepping around the dance floor, was a big crowd of men in boots and cowboy hats and sturdy women who looked as tough and weathered as the men. It was 2008, but you did not have to squint to imagine it might be 1958 or some more distant year.

Connie moved easily among these ranchers and their wives. Shouting over the music, he swapped stories with craggy-faced men who knew him from their rodeo days. Thick-waisted women in advanced middle age smiled like schoolgirls when he asked them to dance. I took a turn myself with a local gal who was deeply amused by my fumbling two step. Connie watched and nodded his approval at my willingness to dive right in.

While the rest of us ordered more beer and whiskey, Connie made an early exit. He'd been up since before sunrise and knew another dawn was not far away.

Late the next morning, we formed a caravan of trucks, campers and horse trailers and headed north out of town. As the miles rolled by, we went from asphalt to gravel to dirt roads. We passed through the tiny town of Whitewater, a solitary place with a grain elevator, a scattering of very modest homes and a school with 50 students – kindergarten through 12th grade. And we kept going and going, past farms and ranches, up muddy hills and through slippery gumbo that spattered windshields and packed thick on the underbellies of our trucks.

Finally, the dirt road ran out and we simply followed ruts worn in the prairie. Down a grassy slope, through a barbed-wire gate and just past a pond that reflected the cloudy, steel gray sky, we came to a lonesome corral in the middle of nowhere.

Except it wasn't nowhere. It was a far pasture among the 29,000 acres of the ZN Ranch – the ranch Connie had bought back in the winter of 1968, the home where he raised his two sons and one daughter, the dream ranchland he spotted from an airplane on his way from a Canadian rodeo and the place from which he would be exiled by a divorce.

On that first afternoon as we set up camp, all that I could see of the land was wide rolling prairie, just like the endless miles of flat ranching country I had driven through along the Highline – Highway 2 – all the way from Great Falls. But a little gully stretching down from where Connie set up the hand-built portable toilet gave a hint of something beyond; rockier ground and a high mesa in the distance.

The horses were set free to roam, as they would be each night. At daybreak, Paul Masson would ride out to gather the little herd and drive them back to the corral. Paul, the guy who first told me about Connie and the ZN Ranch, is a transplanted Californian who has a small compound in Monroe, just outside of Seattle, where he keeps his horses. He was just another guest when he first came to the ZN but has graduated to become Connie's chief wrangler for the yearly roundup.

Most mornings, I tried to be out of my tent before Paul and the horses thundered by. Typically, though, I'd fall behind schedule and end up in a rush to get myself organized, find my horse and saddle up. I'd be fumbling with my chaps or taking a quick stop at the outdoor toilet or running back for something I left in my tent or struggling to get the bit in my horse's mouth and I'd look up and see Connie riding slowly away from camp. Penny Nicholls informed me early on that Connie was prone to do that. Not a man to order people around, he just figures everyone will be ready when they are supposed to be ready and he just goes when he goes. Somehow, I would always catch up, Connie would say no word of disapproval, and the adventure would begin.

The morning of that first day, we traversed the prairie and came to a sudden cliff that fell away into a maze of coulees and a lovely valley bisected by the meandering Frenchman Creek. When Connie first rode this land back in '67, he could see that the high grass around the creek and the hidden corners of the coulees would provide perfect winter feed and shelter for cattle.

Riding into the valley, I felt time slipping away. Other than a few abandoned homesteaders' shacks and the fence line at the top of the ridge, there was no sign of civilization. The place has not changed in a hundred years. Maybe 10,000. Look close at a big rock and discover it is petrified wood. In sandy areas, find seashells left behind by an ancient ocean.

Cattle can disappear in a place like this and the big challenge is finding every last cow and calf pair. They wander up high cliffs that are capped by soft ground where a horse can sink to his belly. They hover in the thicket where a horseman has a devil of a time following. They cross the muddy creek and a cowboy has to cross, as well, to bring them back. Our job was to go into all those places, gather the cattle together and drive them up the coulees to the flat pastures above. Whenever we thought we had them all, Connie's son, Clinton, would do a flyover of the ranch he now runs and come back to tell us, with a sly smile, we had missed a pair. Dutifully, we'd head back down to look for the mavericks, wanting to prove ourselves as something more than useless city folk on holiday. We knew, of course, that Clinton could do our work in half the time with just his horse and a couple of eager dogs

During my first visit to the ZN, I expended a lot of energy chasing cows and pushing them as hard as I could. I wore myself out, wore out my horse and probably annoyed the cattle. By my fourth year, I finally paid attention to how Connie did the job: slow and easy. He is never in a rush. Once, when we were riding out, he asked me why I kept urging my horse into a lope. I came up with some phony explanation, but, the truth was, I was doing it for fun.

Somehow, I knew that would seem pretty ridiculous to Connie. There was a job to be done and using up a horse just for the fun of it was a rookie's mistake.

But, as I said, Connie never lectured me. One time, after I had learned just enough about throwing a rope to be dangerous, I was helping Connie move some calves into a pen. One calf kept running off, so I got the bright idea that I could rope him. I twirled the lariat over my head, tossed it in the direction of the calf and, to my amazement, it dropped right over his ears and around his throat – at which point he took off running and yanked the rope right out of my hand. All Connie said was, "I guess you need to figure out how to get that rope back." If he was upset, he did not show it – even though it was *his* rope.

One of Connie's favorite bits of philosophy, and one he repeats often, is "I would rather you watch and do than for me to instruct and tell." He is gratified when you finally notice the right way to do things, but, like letting the cows find their own pace on a cattle drive, he will patiently wait for the light to dawn in the brain of an aspiring ranch hand.

"I've thought for 20 years, it's a poor day when you can't learn something if you listen and watch," he said.

He applies that to himself, as well as to those who can learn from him. One morning, I was warming up my horse with some rudimentary groundwork, trying to get him used to me. Connie watched for a while. Then he sauntered over to ask what I was doing. I felt a little embarrassed, certain I was doing something incorrectly. But then I realized this man who had ridden horses since he was a child was asking a sincere question. In his eighth decade, still looking to learn more, he thought that even I might have a new trick to show him. The fact that I actually had absolutely nothing to teach him about horses simply demonstrates how Connie is not a guy who assumes he knows it all and has nothing left to learn.

Connie has hosted hundreds of guests over the years from all over the United States and other parts of the planet. "What I have learned by listening and watching the guests is worth as much or more than the money I've made," he said. Unlike the typical dude ranch operator, he doesn't spend his time worrying about insurance claims and disasters waiting to happen. He matches each guest to a horse and then lets them go. Riding with Connie comes as close to being a real cowboy as most of us are ever going to get. We cover treacherous ground in search of cattle. We grab hot irons from a roaring fire and wade into the chaos of branding day. We head off alone when the mood strikes us. As raw and unskilled as we may be, at the end of the day we feel the exhausted satisfaction of having done a real job the best we can.

Connie allows this to happen because we are not customers; we are his newest friends. He gets a lot of joy from sharing his world with eager outsiders and he does not judge them because they lack the skills he has acquired over a lifetime. One saying he likes is, "Never judge a cowboy by what he wears. Some that look the part are not and some that don't, are." A person does not have to live a life just like his to earn Connie's respect.

At some point during each day, Connie will say, "Boy, this is livin'!" It might be in the middle of a rainstorm or when we have just come down a steep ravine where the horses struggled to find a hold in the muddy ground, but he does not say it with irony. He means it. This is living for him; the only life he has ever wanted.

"I guess a person is lucky, a fella told me, if you're making a living at what you're doing and you like it. I had an adopted brother and I got along with him. He married an Indian lady and they had five or six kids and he was a janitor and drove a bus and he was as happy as could be.

"I was born to it. Just because I like it don't mean everybody does. You know, ranching people, everybody here, likes it, but very few people would want to make a living at it. Sure, yesterday was beautiful. But when it's 30 below and you're feeding cows and your tractor breaks down or your horse breaks down and you got five cows over here on a ridge and you spend all day getting 'em back in and its cold, cold, cold – well, you have your good points and your bad points to everything."

For Connie, even the "cold, cold, cold" could not outweigh the good points of a life in the saddle. To watch him mount up and ride is to witness a transformation. Connie is living proof of Will Rogers' often-repeated words: "The outside of a horse is good for the inside of a man."

Horses have been his work partners. Horses have been his recreation. Horses have allowed him passage into the deeper reaches of the West. Without horses, the story of Connie's life would be utterly different; the horses he has used to herd cattle, the many broncs he rode to notoriety in the rodeo – and the two horses he took with him when he ran away from his childhood home.

COMPETING
IS FROM THE
NECK DOWN,
BUT WINNING
IS FROM THE
NECK UP.

Sally Tonkin

3 • "WE WERE ALL CRAZY"

Connie says his father was a mean man – mean to his mother, tough on his son. As a young man, Arthur Cox got hung up in the saddle of a running horse, banged his head real hard and failed to go see a doctor. People later figured the ordeal somehow rattled his brain. In later life, he would spend shorts stints in a mental hospital. When he was in his right mind, Connie's dad was a good ranch manager, but then some loose wires in his head would cross and the man would descend into six months of unkindness and anger.

Connie was born in Havre, Montana, on March 21st 1933. The family farmed and ranched 20 miles out of town and Connie learned to ride a horse about 10 minutes after he learned to walk. At age six, he accompanied his dad and some friends on an 80-mile expedition trailing 65 bucking horses to a rodeo in Chester. Connie remembers that long-ago journey well – the three-hour struggle to get the horses to cross a narrow wooden bridge over a river; the mule that had to be dragged across; sharing a bedroll with his father; the bacon and eggs and bread in the morning; the dead mouse discovered in the bottom of the coffee pot at the end of breakfast.

At home, there was a coal stove, an outside bathroom and all the chores that ranch kids do that add up to a cowboy education. In third and fourth grade, Connie was sent into town for school. He hated it. He preferred the solitude of life on the ranch.

"I would've made a good hillbilly if I hadn't got out into the world," he said.

At the age of 15, Connie could no longer tolerate his dad's cruelties. Riding one horse and leading another, he made the trek to his uncle and aunt's home and there he stayed. He only went back to visit his mother when he knew his dad was not around.

Free of his father, he still felt trapped by painful social awkwardness.

"I was ungodly shy," Connie said. "I was bashful. Oh, you wouldn't believe it. I hated it when I started high school… Being shy, being bashful – it's terrible, it's horrible and I had to break myself of it, so I started telling jokes."

He memorized every joke, humorous story and tall tale he could stuff into his brain. Humor gave him an opening into conversations and the conversations led to friendships. Some of those jokes still get a re-telling to all who sit by his gasoline-soaked campfires.

Young Connie made a stab at all kinds of jobs. "I used to work as a kid riding the colts in the sale ring in the fall," he told me. "I worked on the railroad six months; I hated that. I worked construction six months; I hated that. In the wintertime I helped put up ice. The only thing I liked is what we're doing today" -- another day of riding and moving cattle.

He never expected a life of riches and, in that, he has not been disappointed. "I've always been in debt since I was 19 years old," Connie said. But, at 20, he did have the five bucks needed to enter his first rodeo. That was on a rainy day in May 1953 in Maple Creek, Saskatchewan. He walked away with third place in bareback riding, a fourth in cow riding and $35 in winnings. It would not be long before the paydays got richer and the first place belt buckles began to accumulate.

In 2009, my son Daniel and I were at Connie's house in Deer Lodge where he was managing the Burnt Hollow Ranch and hosting guest riders a couple of weeks during the summer. A few of his buckles were on display and he pulled open a drawer filled with a whole lot more. A rough count put the total at 85. I tried to get him to talk about his rodeo championships, but he evaded my questions. The best cowboys do not brag about their prowess and Connie passed it all off as if it were a hobby no more worthy of note than collecting stamps.

It took a special trip to Montana to uncover some of Connie's rodeo history.

In late November 2011, I boarded the train in Seattle and rode overnight to Havre. Connie was waiting for me at the station. We climbed into his pickup and drove across town to the Eagles hall for a reunion he had organized with many of the rodeo veterans with whom he once traveled the circuit throughout Montana, up into Alberta and Saskatchewan, down into Wyoming and California and to scattered states and provinces beyond. All these men had settled into ranching and decades of hearty meals had settled around many a belly, but their memories of the glory days of reckless youth were not forgotten. If their stories can be believed, the wildest of this wiry wild bunch was the once-bashful Connie Cox.

Competing in a rodeo is, by definition, risky behavior. It is a sport for the impulsive, no the cautious. And, apparently, for a painfully shy young man, it was a world in which he could bust loose. After the competition was over, the cowboys would head from the chutes to the saloons. The hard drinking would begin and the pranks would ensue. Connie's friend, Ed Solomon, remembers one of Connie's tavern tricks. "We used to pull some really dumb things," he said. "Connie would get down on the floor and crawl up behind a girl and bite her on the leg." Heck of a way to meet a gal.

Early on, Connie learned to pilot a small airplane as quick transportation across the wide open spaces. On one occasion, Connie was urging Solomon to fly to a rodeo with him, but Solomon said he just could not do it. He had a field of alfalfa to cut and no time for running off to a rodeo. Try as he might, Connie could not convince his friend to go and so, on the day of departure, Ed was out on his John Deere, skimming through the alfalfa.

"Pretty soon," Solomon recalled, "there comes this kind of cloud over me, a shadow, and my hat flew off and went ahead of me. And it came down that the wheel of Connie's plane knocked my hat off. He did a kind of flip-flop and flew on down the road. That was a little too close. He's crazier than hell, that's what I thought."

Crazier still was the time Cox and Solomon were fooling around in the airplane up along the Canadian border. A pair of military jets dropped in to warn them away. As a joke Connie put the airplane into a steep dive and turned off the engine. As the airplane went into a tailspin, Connie leaned back and asked Ed if he was ready to quit the dive. Ed replied, "No, Connie, you're going to hit the ground first."

Miraculously, Connie managed to pull up at the last moment, but the aircraft clipped the top of a fence and mangled the propeller.

"We were all crazy, I guess, but he pulled more goofy stuff," Solomon said. "He had a lot of talent though. He was a good hand."

No one at the reunion disputed that. In fact, most said Connie was among the best Montana rodeo riders of his day. "He did all of the events and he was good at all of them," Wade Bickford said. Bickford has known Connie since they were in grade school together. He does recall Connie once scaring a riding partner half to death by pretending to pass out on the back of his loping horse. And he has a tale to tell about an insane flight from the Jordan Rodeo in the middle of a howling storm, but he said Connie always took things seriously inside the rodeo arena.

Well, almost always.

There was a younger attendee at the reunion named Dick Grannell who played a role in one of Connie's grandest pranks. Dick now is a stocky rancher who would not be mistaken for anything but a red-blooded American male. But four decades ago he was a slim, teenage ranch hand who worked for Connie and the man who was Connie's closest companion on the rodeo circuit, Merle Boyce. Merle and Connie figured if teenaged Dick was dressed up just right, well, he might possibly pass for a cowgirl.

The person who inspired this lunatic idea was a celebrated lady bronc rider from Indianapolis named Roseanna Green. Merle and Connie had met Roseanna in Indiana and they thought it would fun to bring her west for a rodeo. And, if not her, then someone they could pass off as her.

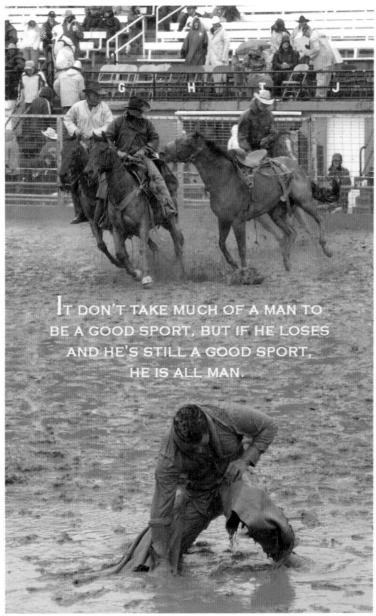

It don't take much of a man to be a good sport, but if he loses and he's still a good sport, he is all man.

Connie and Dick were flying to the rodeo in Winnifred, Montana, one June day at the start of the 1960s when Connie told young Dick to look inside a sack in the back of the plane. Inside the sack, Dick found a blonde wig, a fancy cowgirl shirt and fire-engine-red, bell-bottom riding pants. Dick wanted to know what the gear was for.

"Me and Merle decided that with all this talk going around about Roseanna Green, she needs to come out here from Indiana and actually show everybody just how good she can ride," Connie told Dick. "Well, she can't make it, so you're going to be Roseanna."

Dick, as crazy as Merle and Connie, said he would do it and, amazingly, the trick worked. With the help of two female accomplices, Dick was dressed up, made up and fixed up with two big balloons tucked inside his snazzy shirt. Apparently, he fooled everybody, including the father of a girl he had been wooing. Boyce and Cox spread the rumor that the lovesick Roseanna Green had come to find Connie in Montana only to be crushed to learn he was married. To compensate, she had entered the saddle bronc competition and intended to go home with the winnings.

"Roseanna" did ride that day. Dick in his Roseanna disguise might well have won, but his cinch broke in mid-ride and, still solid in the saddle, he slid right over the horse's head and down into the dirt. With a quick adjustment to his flopping balloons, Dick maintained the ruse, accepted the applause and Connie had a story to tell for years to come.

Even if your cinch stays in place, every rodeo cowboy knows that being thrown from a bucking animal and landing in the dust is inevitable. Some get tossed more than others, though, and Connie had the experience less than most. Riding saddle broncs, he was bucked off four or five times a year, which is a pretty good record. More impressive, in the 17 years he rode bareback, he was dumped just five times. For about five or six years, from the mid-1950s on, Connie was one of the best cowboys on the Montana amateur circuit. Besides the bronc riding, he competed in calf roping, team roping and bulldogging. He tried bull riding, but it was not his event.

"I got on a few bulls," he said, "but I was scared shitless. I was shivering and shaking like a dog shitting shingle nails."

The rest he enjoyed, despite the injuries that are part of the game. On July 3, 1956, at the rodeo in Choteau, Montana, Connie was aboard another bareback. Coming out of the chute, the horse rubbed the gate and Connie's foot got jammed and bent backwards. He spent that night at the home of Rowena and Vic Sargent, his aunt and uncle, where he kept his leg elevated and iced. The next day, he was back at the rodeo grounds. Someone poured ether on his swollen ankle and foot and forced it into his boot and he got back on another bucking horse.

"Cowboys are a romantic lot and Connie was the best," Aunt Rowena recalled in a letter, telling the story of that day.

The romantic cowboy broke a leg bronc riding in 1956. In '68, his ribs took a beating. "I was bareback riding," he said. "Broke about three ribs where a horse stepped on me. That's the worst. You can't laugh, you can't turn over, you can't fart."

Still, he was making decent money and contemplating a shot at the professional circuit. He was winning nearly every time he showed up for a rodeo and had multiple amateur championships in bareback broncs and bulldogging. His friends say he could have made it big as a pro; Connie's not convinced.

"I don't know if I'd ever have been that good," he said. "It would've been nice to be a champion and I had a good opportunity when I was right in my prime in '55. I was 22. But I saw so many of those older guys that were champions for five or six or seven years and they didn't have a pot to piss in and I thought to myself, 'I've got an old man to take care of,'" – his future self – "so that's why I didn't do it."

He also had somebody else to take care of. One of his rodeo buddies, Bob Sivertsen, had a nice looking little sister with auburn hair. Connie started courting her and, on June 1, 1957, he and Marjorie Sivertsen were wed.

"I was a virgin 'till I was 24," Connie claims, "and I was with my wife and she was a virgin and she was 18. We were kissing and neither one of us knew what to do. And she said, 'ain't you goin' any further?' We got up and put our clothes on and went to another town."

That's the way Connie slips a funny line into a recollection of real life. But, joking aside, the bashful boy and his bride did figure out what comes after the kissing. Three children came along quickly – Casey in 1958, Clinton in 1959 and Charlene in 1960. With his growing family, Connie was now ranching a section of land north of Havre that he'd gotten from his grandfather. The wild rodeo days were winding down. A ranching dream was about to come true.

RODEO DAYS: IMAGES FROM CONNIE COX'S CAREER ON THE MONTANA RODEO CIRCUIT

DURING HIS RODEO CAREER, CONNIE DID IT ALL AND DID IT WELL -- ROPING CALVES RIDING BAREBACK BRONCS AND SADDLE BRONCS, STEER WRESTLING (ALSO CALLED BULLDOGGING) AND TEAM ROPING. HE TRIED BULL RIDING A COUPLE OF TIMES BUT DECIDED IT WAS TOO RISKY FOR A MAN WHO PLANNED TO LIVE TO A RIPE OLD AGE.

ROPING AT THE MEADOW LAKE RODEO, 1970. (ABOVE)

RIDING BAREBACK IN JORDAN, 1966. (RIGHT)

BULLDOGING IN LEWISTOWN, 1969. (OPPOSITE)

CONNIE HAZING FOR MIKE EATON
AS HE BRINGS DOWN A STEER AT
THE RODEO IN WOOD MOUNTAIN,
SASKATCHEWAN, IN JULY, 1971.

CONNIE RIDES HIGH ON A SADDLE BRONC.

AT THE LEWISTOWN RODEO IN 1970,
CONNIE ADDED TO HIS BIG COLLECTION
OF FIRST PLACE BELT BUCKLES AND
TOOK HOME $445 IN WINNINGS.

IN 1967 IN LEWISTOWN, CONNIE RODE IN
HIS BEST EVENT: BAREBACK BRONCS.
(OPPOSITE)

THROUGH TWO
DECADES OF
COMPETITION IN
RODEOS, BOTH
IN THE UNITED
STATES AND
CANADA, CONNIE
ACQUIRED A LONG
LIST OF GREAT
FRIENDS. HERE
ARE JUST A FEW
OF THEM...

LARRY KANE RIDES BRONCS AT THE SIDNEY, IOWA RODEO, 1972 (OPPOSITE) AND IN FORT WORTH, TEXAS, IN 1966.

GARTH BASCOM BRAVES THE BULLS IN LEWISTOWN IN 1968 AND JO ANN GEE RACES AROUND THE BARRELS AT THE 1972 STATE FINALS IN PLAINS.

CHICK SMITH BARREL RACING AT SAN FRANCISCO'S COW PALACE IN 1978.

BRONC RIDER JIM MURPHY AT THE LEWISTOWN STETSON STAMPEDE.

AT A RODEO IN ALBERTA, ROPER TOBY KNUTSON HEADS A STEER.

JOHN GEE
BULLDOGS OFF
A FAMOUS HORSE
NAMED POPCORN.

LOUIE SHEPP
TAKES A WILD
RIDE AT THE
TOWNSEND
RODEO IN 1968.

JIM MURPHY ON
A BULL NAMED
HIGH POCKETS,
WINNETT
RODEO, 1966.

AT THE RODEO IN ROUNDUP ON THE 4TH OF JULY, 1975, AMOS CHARBONNEAU AND CHARLIE PHILLIPS TEAM UP TO ROPE A STEER.

DON GREYTAK LEADS A HORSE NAMED BUCK IN CHINOOK, 1962.

DICK GRANNELL FLIES OUT OF THE SADDLE BEFORE A CROWD IN LEWISTOWN IN 1968.

CONNIE'S RODEO DAYS BROUGHT PLENTY OF REWARDS, WILD TIMES AND ROUGH THRILLS, BUT HE KNEW EARLY ON THAT HE WANTED SOMETHING MORE -- SOMETHING LIKE WHAT HIS FRIEND, RAY PEARSON, FOUND UP IN MANYBERRIES, ALBERTA: A BIG RANCH TO CALL HIS OWN.

"The outside of a horse is good, for the inside of a man."
― WILL ROGERS

4 • THE ZN

On the 4th of July, 1969, at the rodeo in Roundup, Montana, Connie took one of his final bareback rides. His buddy, Ed Solomon, was the pick up man. (For the uninitiated, the pick up man is the rider who comes alongside to help a successful competitor make a more comfortable exit from a bucking animal.) Connie had completed his eight second ride and was now looking for the pick up to come get him off the bucking bronc.

"Ed just sat on his horse and laughed at me," Connie recalled, "and pretty soon I fell off."

Cox and Solomon were still up to their old antics, but rodeo was no longer a priority. Serious ranching was the new passion.

Flying back from rodeos in Sakatchewan in the late 1960s, Connie would cross the border and look down to see an attractive stretch of ground below – grassland, coulees, high ridges and a narrow valley with a stream cutting a winding path through it all. It was the ZN Ranch.

It happened that the son of the couple who owned the ranch lived in Havre and Connie knew him. On Dec. 27, 1967, during a winter with little snow, Connie, Margie and a banker, along with the ranchers' son and his wife, drove out to the ZN to take a look. Connie and the banker liked what they saw. After dinner, they got down to business. The owners were in their mid-sixties. The woman was tired of living 65 miles from Malta, the nearest substantial town. Connie offered them 29 percent down on a price of $190,000. The woman pointed her finger at Connie and asked if he could really do that. Connie said he had his banker right outside, backing the deal.

Connie spent the next three days riding the ranch, still liking what he saw. In January, they reconvened with their lawyers at a bowling alley in Havre and signed the papers. When Connie thanked the owners' lawyer for his time, he told Connie he was surprised the couple went through with the agreement.

"When she wanted to sell, he didn't want to sell and when he wanted to sell, she didn't want to sell," Connie remembers the lawyer saying.

The section of land Connie got from his grandfather covered the down payment. The rest would have to come from good luck and hard work. "It was tough," Connie said. "I did everything but run a whorehouse."

Three times, the family trailed cattle from Havre to the ZN up along the Canadian border – about 120 miles. "The boys were little," Connie said. "Margie would come along with a camper on the pickup and she'd cook for us. We got 'em down here pretty cheap."

The Cox kids enrolled at the tiny school in Whitewater and Connie went to work "ranching and building up and cutting more cows" across the 29,000 acres of his new home. It was, he believed, the thing he was born to do.

Connie knew it costs more to run cattle on flat land. One of the attributes he saw in the ZN Ranch was the rough terrain. The cattle could largely fend for themselves down in the coulees that spill into the valley of Frenchman Creek. "Down there, if the winter is right, it's not tough," he said. "You save that for winter range and it doesn't cost as much to run 'em. You don't have to feed 'em as much, you let 'em run on their own."

For Connie and Margie, these were the golden years of building a ranch and raising a family. In 1973, they put up a new ranch house. Next to the big red barn, they built a big arena where the children could practice roping. That developed into an annual clinic for team roping. "I had a kind of school with a jackpot afterwards that went on for six days," Connie said, "and we had 150 team ropers come." The "school" lasted 20 years.

Just as suburban parents drive their kids all over town for soccer games and gymnastics tournaments, Connie and Margie covered many miles in Montana taking their sons and daughter to roping competitions. In a letter written to a friend in 1990 – after the children were grown and grandchildren had come along – Margie described those roping days:

"The kids have given us some great moments in our lives. They started young and won in the NRA, College, and Casey qualifying for the National Pro-Rodeo Cowboys' Association Finals in 1988, at Las Vegas, Nevada!

"This isn't anything that a lot of other people haven't done, but they had to do it on their own. They bought their own horses and when Casey was 15, he went roping all summer and roped against, and with, the top men competitors and had to pay his own way.

"I guess the main thing is they all had the ambition and try instilled in them at an early age by Connie and it seems to have helped them become good citizens. Connie was a great Dad when the kids were growing up – he took all three with him all the time and is now getting to enjoy the grandkids."

According to Charlene, Connie was a loving dad but a tough taskmaster. In that, he was typical of ranching men who set a high standard and a hard line for their kids, a style that is very different from many modern fathers who live

FLYING SOUTH FROM RODEOS IN CANADA, CONNIE WOULD CROSS THE BORDER INTO MONTANA AND FOLLOW THE COURSE OF FRENCHMAN CREEK, PEERING DOWN AT AN ALLURING SIGHT BELOW -- THE ZN RANCH.

IN 1968, HE BOUGHT THE RANCH AND SPENT THE NEXT QUARTER CENTURY GROWING HIS CATTLE BUSINESS AND RAISING A FAMILY.

in places where life's edges are more soft and forgiving.

As Clinton grew older, the differences between father and son became sharp and contentious. Connie talks of this estrangement through one of his ever-handy sayings:

"When you're five, your dad's the greatest guy in the world. When you're 12 or 13, he's all right for a dollar bill now and them. From the time you're 17 through 24 that's when he's the dumbest son of a bitch in the world. By the time you're 40, it's 'Well, dad used to say…'"

Still, though Casey and Charlene grew up and moved away, Clinton stayed close. Ranching was in his blood as much as it was in his father's. Connie now says Clinton is twice the rancher he ever was – a better mechanic, a better businessman, "he's putting up more hay, his cows are bigger."

Connie did well enough, though. Through the cycling seasons of calving, branding, cutting hay, moving the herd to new pastures, testing new breeds, watching beef prices rise and drop, gathering the cattle in the fall and shipping them to market – through all the endless labor, busted machinery, sick animals and fences in need of repair, Connie stuck with it. The ZN was his kingdom and, even on the coldest, hardest days, he was living the life he loved.

Growing up at the ZN Ranch, all three of Connie's children became skilled in the saddle. Here, a young Charlene and an even younger Clinton test those skills in competition.

Clinton Cox now runs the ZN Ranch. It is home for him, his daughters, Macey and Calli and his wife, Denise.

CALLI (RIGHT) AND MACEY (UPPER RIGHT) HAVE GROWN UP AT THE ZN TAKING A HAND IN ALL PARTS OF RANCH LIFE. AT BRANDING TIME, THEIR COUSIN -- CHARLENE'S SON, CASH COLEMAN -- COMES TO HELP ROPE THE CALVES. (ABOVE)

Here's hoping health's the horse under you; ahead, a long easy ride.
Good water and grass to the top of the pass where the trails cross the Big Divide.

— CHARLES M. RUSSELL

5 • THE BIG DRIVE OF '89

While apprentice cowboys like me dream of doing, for just a few days, the things real cowboys do, real cowboys like Connie Cox dream of doing the big things the westerners of old once did. They envy the men who first came to Montana on the great cattle drives of the 19th century. If they had the opportunity to do something as grand, they would jump at the chance.

In 1989, Connie Cox got his chance. That year marked the 100th anniversary of Montana's statehood. A few years prior, someone had come up with the idea of commemorating the occasion by drawing together a huge herd of cattle, assembling a wagon train and inviting cowboys, cowgirls, ranchers and any camp followers who cared to come along to take part in a giant cattle drive. Committees were formed, corporate sponsors were found and a route was picked. The drive would end in Montana's biggest city, Billings. The assembly point would be farther north in Roundup near the old terminus point of many of the legendary drives that came up from Texas to open the state to cattle ranching.

When the Great Montana Centennial Cattle Drive of 1989 was announced, skeptics thought the enterprise was too ambitious. They expected it to collapse under the heavy weight of a thousand complications. It certainly would not come off if there were not enough eager dreamers, damn fools and top hands willing to sign on. Connie happily volunteered. He figured, even if nobody else showed up at the rendezvous point, he could just keep heading on to Billings where he'd sell his cows. There was nothing to lose by trying and a lot of regret to live with if he failed to go.

"Some say that 'The Big Drive of '89' to celebrate Montana's 100th birthday of statehood will never take place," Connie wrote at the start of the journal he kept during the journey, "but we'll not know unless we try. So we're putting this set of longhorn cows south down the trail with the faith that two years of planning by a lot of good Montana people will result in a cattle trek to Billings that will not be forgot."

Connie was confident enough that something big was in the works that, long before he had taken his herd a mile, he had teamed up with a writer, Dr. Jim Scott, and a photographer, Cal Sorenson, to produce a book about the event, told from his own perspective. That book, "Epic Trails: Endless Tracks Across the Centuries," may not have proved to be the smartest business venture (books are even chancier than ranching), but it stands as a testament to the fact

37

that the centennial drive was, in many ways, the crowning achievement of Connie's cowboy career and the most glorious 34 days of his life.

The official drive from Roundup to Billings would cover 60 miles. If all went as planned, there would be plenty of company and elaborate logistical support for that stretch. Connie's bigger challenge was moving more than 100 longhorns on his own to Roundup from the ZN Ranch near the Saskatchewan border -- a much longer trail of 240 miles. Planning a route was no simple matter, given that the open, empty range of 1889 is now mostly fenced, private land. He made arrangements for passage and pasture with ranchers all along the way. He gathered a herd, assembled a revolving crew of drovers and prepared to be gone from home for more than a month.

On Friday, August 11, 1989 at 6:45 a.m., Connie began moving his cows south along Frenchman Creek. The sky was clear; the temperature was in the 90s. That first day he covered 15 miles.

Each day, Connie kept a record of the journey. His account of day two is typical:

"Up and gone at 5:45 a.m. Cows trailing good. Stop for breakfast at 10 a.m. Cows are trailing about 2 to 3 miles per hour. Watered cows at Hilmer and Edna Bakke's and let them rest 'til about 1:30 p.m. Got to Milk River bridge at 3 p.m. and had a lot of trouble trying to get them to cross bridge. After more than 1 ½ hour of refusing to take the bridge, Carl Stahl brought some hay and scattered it on the approach and on bridge. Cows followed across in just a few minutes and were all across by nearly 4:30. Let them water again at Milk River and corralled cows for overnight at Saco Roping Arena."

All along the route, old friends and new acquaintances came to help for a few hours or a few days. They brought their children and grandchildren to ride along. Mosquitoes buzzed in, rattlesnakes slithered by. A few cows got foot-sore and lame. Mistakes were made. Horses got loose and had to be chased down. Accidents happened and crew members were carted off to the doctor. Dogs got lost and found again. The wagon broke down and got repaired. And, through it all, the land and sky surrounded Connie and company with grandeur.

"Sun rose over the ridge at 6:24 this morning," Connie wrote on day nine. "Last night was beautiful. Big moon, lots of stars. Slept good… Little Rocky Mountains look really close this morning. Sure are a pretty sight."

On the trail, there was plenty of time for reflection:

"Sunday morning. Lot of people will go to church today. Of those maybe 5 percent would be on the square and you could depend on them if needed to go to the end of the road with you. In our crew we have five people and we all would go to the end of the road together, 100% for each other. Beautiful morning. Little Rockies off to the northwest – Breaks in the south – and Judith Mountains way south across the Missouri. No wind and about 60 degrees above. Man never had a church as beautiful as God made this. As Bruce and I sit on our horses and with hat in our hands, give thanks, we are truly blessed. Time is 6:32 a.m."

On day 11, Connie realized this was the longest he had ever trailed cattle, eclipsing the 10 days he, Margie and the kids had spent moving their herd from Havre to their new home at the ZN in 1969. "Lots of ways, seems like it was only yesterday, and other times, seems a hundred years ago. Good to think back on those things."

Connie also thought back to the men who preceded him a century before:

"Went to Zortman for supper and to get fuel. Old time trail hands did not have choice of pickup nor trailer to go back for crippled stock or scout new territory… Those old time cowboys would think we were sure a bunch of 'greeners.' I think I'd have liked their ways better."

After a surprisingly easy bridge crossing over the Missouri River, Connie ruminated further on the pioneering cattlemen:

"Sure was a pretty sight with the wagon, saddle stock and cattle all strung out coming down the hill and crossing the bridge. Smooth as our crossing went compared to what we expected it could have been, sure made me think how relieved those old timers must have been when they had to swim their stock or get through bogs or quicksand before finally making a safe crossing. Times some of them didn't make it. For many, their only monument to have been a drover on one of those historic early drives was a lonesome grave with a crude wooden marker along the banks of the North Platte, Canadian, Yellowstone or some other river like the Missouri which claimed them."

Weather in Montana is a fickle thing. Sun and blue sky can transform in an eye blink into hard rain and cold wind. On the trail to Roundup, this proved to be as true as ever. "Mother Nature is a beautiful lady most of the time and real good to us, but once in a while she can be a real bitch and make life miserable when she chooses," Connie wrote on day 17. "Sometimes she doesn't want to give you much warning when she decides to throw one of her temper tantrums either."

The morning of day 18 was cold and wet. "Camp very muddy. Can't move. Cows reluctant to get up from spot they've warmed on the wet ground for their beds. Can really see the steam of their breathing in the chilly dawn air. Horses and crew all standing around with hump in their backs and shivering to warm up. Will eat breakfast early while we wait for mud to dry enough to break camp. Bruce is cook this morning. Warmed us up good with coffee, bacon, eggs, potatoes with onions and bread. Finally got the kinks out and got cows to trailing about ten after 9 a.m."

As Connie's expedition drew near to Roundup, the spooked cows balked at crossing a bridge. A shallow crossing was found three miles south, but, at that point, the route became confusing. Attempting to get back on track, Connie came across the single person he had encountered along the way who was slow to offer help:

"Talked with a Hutterite by name of Ken Stahl and he first said, 'Don't think ya can get to Roundup from here with your cattle.'

"I asked him if there wasn't some way around a couple more times and kept getting the same reply... You shoulda seen him grin and his eyes light up when I asked him one more time and just happened to let him get a bit of a glimpse of a twenty I'd pulled from my pocket! 'Oh, yah, yah, I think ya can get from here to Roundup with your cows all right!' He then proceeded to give detailed directions which way to go."

After three weeks of trailing, Connie arrived at Roundup. It was a bustling scene. Cattle were being trucked in from around the state. Wagons were arriving from all over Montana, Alberta, Saskatchewan and from as far away as Texas. The feedlots were full. Traffic was backed up on the roads near the registration tents. TV crews swarmed. Tourists snapped pictures.

Connie and his companions went to the rodeo where he saw old friends. Afterwards, they strolled to the Maverick Bar to "see if we can't wash some of the trail dust down. Didn't make it back to camp until 3:15 a.m."

A photograph of Connie appeared in the Billings Gazette. "From the looks of my picture it appears I've shrunk a little since we left home. Found a scale and weighed. Weight – 174 pounds. Have lost 14 pounds on the trail so far. My horse, 'Blue,' is looking a little like a greyhound, too."

On Monday, Sept. 4 – Labor Day – the centennial drive began and Connie was raring to go:

"Up early! The biggest day in the history of Roundup is about to begin. About the biggest day in history ever far as I'm concerned and know plenty of folks around here feel the same way I do this morning. Wranglers have been jingling horses from Collins' pens since hours before daylight. Everybody getting their wagons hitched up. Drovers across the river have main herd bunching and moving toward south end of field where they'll start them out on the trail. Cavalry outfit is all trim and ready for parade. You can see 'Old Glory' lots of places – riders carryin' her and Stars and Stripes flying from several wagons. Makes it kind of hard to swallow – keep having to wipe dust or something out of eyes.

"About 2,700 head of cattle in main herd, some 300 more to lead wagon train of more than 200 wagons and some 3,500 saddle horses and riders out of Roundup...

"Parade started for Roundup at 10:45 a.m. Leachman's herd of big horned cattle go first. Our longhorns follow 30 minutes later, then the wagons start to roll. Thousands of people lined up to see the parade go through town...

"Darrel Adolph, Amos Charbonneau and myself moved out in front of our cows and they held nicely as they trailed through that canyon of spectators lining the street. We had about 20 other cowboys and cowgirls riding along to flank the sides and follow behind to keep cows together. This crew made me proud in spirit with their quiet, assured capability as we moved ahead of the wagon train and big mob of riders. Still having problem with dust getting in eyes…

"All I know is if I live to be a hundred years old, I'll never be able to fully describe the feelings that are deep inside. What a great day! And it is actually taking place. It is happening!"

The drive on to Billings was very different from the run from Frenchman Creek. This was a huge, rolling festival. At the encampment each night there were portable showers, caterers, a big Busch beer tent with cowboy poets and musicians performing and thousands of civilians jamming up the roads to drop in for the party. When a stagecoach or wagon tipped over, a helicopter flew in to evacuate the injured. Connie's longhorns were melded with the rest of the giant herd. Free of responsibilities as a trail boss, he worked like any other cowboy, helping move wagons over steep hills and loping ahead to open gates and take down fences so the great caravan could roll on through. He lost his spare clothes, his trail bag and his bedroll, but managed to hang on to his hat, his saddle and Blue.

Near the end, before the grand parade into Billings, Connie rode to the crest of a hill and looked out at the long line of cattle, cowboys, cowgirls, wagons, mules and horses that stretched for two-and-a-half miles in both directions.

"What a beautiful sight!" he wrote in his journal. "Blue seems to sense it, too, as he stands motionless and lets me just sit there for a long time to look and watch this spectacular, grand sight. I doubt I will ever get to see anything like this again and I don't think anyone else will either. This is as close to Heaven on this Earth as man will get to. Words can't express what I felt as I saw one of the last wagons making the climb behind me and watched its crew proudly swinging their 4 horse hitch of big matched roans easily around a sharp turn and I could see the ripple of their American flag as the Stars and Stripes waved out from its place on their wagon as it has this entire drive."

On Sept. 13th, 34 days after leaving home, the adventure was over. With his cattle sold and new clothes bought to replace those he lost, Connie climbed into his pickup for the 300-mile journey to Frenchman Creek. "I do have mixed emotions as I drive north on Highway 87. Glad I'm going home and sorry it is all over."

I CANNOT SEE. I CANNOT PEE.
I CANNOT CHEW. I CANNOT SCREW.
MY MEMORY SHRINKS. MY HEARING STINKS.
NO SENSE OF SMELL. I LOOK LIKE HELL.
THE GOLDEN YEARS HAVE COME AT LAST...
THE GOLDEN YEARS CAN KISS MY ASS.

At age 4, success is not peeing in your pants.

At age 12, success is having friends.

At age 17, success is having a driver's license.

At age 35, success is having money.

At age 50, success is having money.

At age 70, success is having a drivers license.

At age 75, success is having friends.

At age 80, success is not peeing in your pants.

6 • FOLLOWING EPIC TRAILS

In the prologue to "Epic Trails: Endless Tracks Across the Centuries," Jim Scott describes his first visit to the ZN Ranch. He makes it sound idyllic: the sunrise washing shadows from the breaks reaching into the vale of Frenchman Creek; partridges roosting in the sagebrush; the switchbacks of a dusty road descending from a hogback ridge down to the ranch compound; the100-year-old round pen, the big red barn, the working corrals, the feed shed, the bunkhouse and the main house tucked in the curl of the creek backed by willows and hay fields beyond. Scott also paints an idealized picture of the life inside that ranch house: a savvy, hard-working rancher creating a livelihood for his family in a rough country; his resilient wife running a homey kitchen where all are welcome and no one leaves hungry; three children raised well and launched in life and grandchildren born into Montana traditions that root them in the land, the work and the skills of ropes and reins and saddles.

On a drive in Connie's pickup a couple of years ago during his exile in Deer Lodge, I asked him what happened to that perfect life Scott described. Connie just said, "Nobody really knows what goes on inside another man's marriage."

In December 1994, Connie and Margie parted ways. As stipulated in the divorce agreement, operation of the ranch was turned over to their son, Clinton. Connie had to leave the ZN behind and find a new home. That proved not to be easy; he would not solidly settle again for 15 years. Luckily, a good woman came along to help him get through the changes and help reshape his life.

Her name was Linda. Born into a ranching family near Havre, she was educated at the elementary school on the Rocky Boy's Indian Reservation. In a photograph, she was a lone little blonde girl among the red-brown faces and black hair of her classmates. Linda grew up riding a horse and learning the basics of ranch life. She married young, raised a family and, eventually, divorced. Connie knew who Linda was, having worked with her father at the stockyards in Havre. He spied her one night at the dance hall where her son played guitar and sang in a band. He asked Linda to dance and then asked her again. One thing led to another and in May 1997, they married.

Connie and Linda's first home was down on Sarpy Creek in the Bighorn country of southeast Montana. Connie was managing a ranch for a rich lawyer from Florida with the understanding that this place would be a home

LINDA COX

AT HOME IN HAVRE...

...CONNIE'S LIFE HAS COME FULL CIRCLE

for life. There was no contract between them, just the kind of handshake agreement that used to be as solid as steel in the West. So, when the lawyer changed his mind, Connie and Linda were forced to move on.

Next, he found a job near Deer Lodge managing the Burnt Hollow Ranch for a wealthy woman from Seattle. That lasted until the woman's son took over and made changes that no longer included Connie.

Finally, Connie decided he was done managing a place for anyone but himself. He and Linda took up full time residence in the ranch house she had kept in the foothills of the Bear Paw Mountains south of Havre. On the next hill above, Linda's son and his family run a productive, well-tended ranch. On the slopes across the valley, Linda's sisters and their husbands run two more ranches. It is a good, grounded place to finally land; a return to the country where a shy boy named Connie got his start in life.

The years of displacement brought disappointments and frustrations, but Connie is not the type of man to cling to the negative. He found a quote from Charles Dickens that well reflects his attitude: "Reflect upon your present blessings, of which every man has many… not on your past misfortunes, of which all men have some."

Instead of dwelling on things gone haywire in his first marriage and his business associations, Connie kept looking for the next great thing and, in the process, found a way to preserve the spark of adventure that had burned so brightly on the centennial cattle drive.

That new direction actually began to take shape before his first marriage dissolved. Following the Big Drive of '89, Margie's brother, Bob Sivertsen had a brainstorm: the cattle drive to Billings was such a success and attracted so many gawkers and tourists, why not organize one every year and charge outsiders a fee to take part? Bob began trailing cattle with paying guests up along the Canadian border each summer and soon brought Connie in on the operation. Fatefully for Connie, one of those paying guests was a hairdresser from Redmond, Washington, named Penny Nicholls.

Penny was the daughter of a prominent veterinarian in the Seattle area who worked with the thoroughbreds at Longacres racetrack. She grew up with cattle and horses and accompanied her dad on calls to doctor animals. Penny rode horses as a girl but let her interest wane in college. By age 40, she had not gotten on the back of a horse for 20 years.

A beauty shop client who had been on one of Bob Sivertsen's cattle drives told her all about it and showed her photographs. That was enough to renew her interest and, a few months later, Penny was in a car with her husband, Norman, and two friends heading to Montana. It took them three days. Feeling as if they had been driving forever into the outskirts of nowhere, they arrived at the ZN. Only Margie was around to greet them. Eventually, an old blue Dodge rolled up and three men got out. Norman turned to Penny, pointed at the scruffiest, most poorly dressed of the three and said, "I guess he works for this place."

Actually, he owned the place. He was Connie.

After that first weeklong cattle drive, Penny was hooked. Connie invited her to come back in October to help drive cattle to market. She did. Then she returned for branding in May. Penny bought a horse, a Suburban and a horse trailer and went back again. At this point, Connie had parted ways with his brother-in-law and had made the cattle drives a side operation of his own. He enjoyed finding horses for the guests, leading the rides and being the colorful trail boss for all the greenhorns, but he was looking for someone else to keep track of money, reservations, food and all the other details. Penny already ran her salon; how hard could it be to manage a week of riding for 10 or 15 guests? In the spring of 1994, she and Connie formed a partnership to run Epic Trails Cattle Drives.

From trailing cattle along the border, Epic Trails evolved into three weeks of riding and working cattle at various ranches. The operation was first based at Sarpy, then moved to Deer Lodge. The most exciting venue was, and still is, roundup week at the ZN. Clinton Cox was at first skeptical about allowing strangers from all over the country to bumble around the ranch, scare the cows, tire the horses, get in the way at branding time and likely injure themselves in the process. Things were still a little raw between him and his dad, as well, and that further dampened his enthusiasm. Still, he let Connie and Penny make camp by a remote corral and run their crazy dude operation every May. Over time, as he saw guests take the work seriously and come back year after year, Clinton shifted from bare tolerance to amused acceptance of these people who seem so eager for a small taste of ranch life.

There are guest ranches all over the West. Some are essentially vacation camps with swimming pools, tennis courts and tightly managed trail rides. Some are expensive retreats with pristine saddles, expertly-trained horses, gourmet meals and four-star accommodations. Many more are working ranches where ranch families host outsiders as a way to pay the bills and keep the property in the family. Connie and Penny's operation is not like any of those.

For Penny, the business seems secondary, almost an excuse to get a bunch of people together and ride. For Connie, the extra money is nice, but the chance to meet new people and let them partake in the joy he felt on the centennial ride is a bigger motivation. The operation is barebones. The food is good and basic. The bathroom facilities are improvised. Sleeping accommodations? Bring your own. At times, it seems as if no one is really in charge. Everyone simply pitches in.

When I tell my friends in Seattle I am heading to Montana, I do not say I am going to a guest ranch, I say I am joining up with friends to move cattle and ride horses – and that is the closest thing to the truth. My most recent visit was in the heat of July. Our encampment was in the trees along Beaver Creek, just a few miles from Connie and Linda's home. The guests included an adventurous young couple from Philadelphia, a novice rider from New York City, a spunky retired lady from California and four of us from Seattle. Most had ridden with Epic Trails before.

Early each morning we headed out to one of the ranches run by Linda's extended family and helped gather cattle on gorgeous, hilly terrain. By late morning when the triple digit heat arrived we would be done. We spent the afternoons sitting by the creek (or *in* the creek). Sometimes, in the cooler evening, some of us would take another exploratory ride. There was always a communal meal and some time sitting in a circle telling jokes and listening to Connie's tall tales. The ranching families would drop by. Songs would be sung, stories told, bonds of friendship formed. It was easy and unstructured; the farthest thing from a cruise ship or a tour bus. No one was on the outside merely observing. No one was expecting to be pampered or served. We were all in it together, sharing something real, doing a bit of honest work alongside some very grounded people who were happy to welcome us into their bucolic lives.

Connie is the man who has made this experience possible. It is not so much by design as it is simply an expression of who he is and what he appreciates about being alive on this fine planet. There is nothing he loves more than to be out in open country on the back of a horse in the company of friends. And, if he loves it so much, why wouldn't someone from Florida or California or Michigan love it as well? And, if they love it, why shouldn't he invite them along for the ride?

Phill Baily – a fine horseman who I count as a good friend – wrote a poem telling the tale of one week we shared at the ZN. His translation of a modern experience into the cadence of an old cowboy song demonstrates that, with a guide like Connie Cox, even a bunch of city slickers can tap into the soul of the mythic West:

Was it Frenchman Creek or the Muddy Milk

That we crossed that late May day?

From the looks of the horses that trailed the bulls,

Coulda been quicksand, I'd say.

The bulls made it down (well, all but one),

We survived with minimal mishap.

And that was the start of the ZN ride;

It got interesting right after that.

"Get a count of those doggies and get it right,

Seventy-three's what we need to bring back."

To the south and the east we trotted with haste,

Runnin' a circle, cuttin' 'em no slack.

Seventy-three pair was what we're lookin' for,

And seventy-three was what we found.

Ready to brand, we ended day one,

And the bottle was passed round and round.

Stories were told and <u>all</u> were true,

Unless they weren't, of course.

We learned that first day from the master of say,

Truth is only told by the horse.

Next day ropes were down and irons were ready,

The wrestlers waited in line.

Ownership now was to be singed on each calf:

7 on the shoulder, 7 on the hind.

C Bar C went on some I do recall,

On the side and not too high.

Something to do with gender, I think,

But I never did figure out why.

Next day we gathered all remaining pairs,

Or so we thought that day.

Then we heard from the boss later that night,

"Three are still out – go back, get those strays."

Three bandit pair had evaded our sight,

Through the steeps, the mud and the rain.

They were cunning, with hearts of bovine deceit,

But our resolve was to play no refrain.

At first light next day our ponies were jingled,

With a long circle now to be rode.

The objective was clear: find those renegade pairs;

And don't return 'till we get the full load.

So, we rode hard and found those elusive cows,

Darn near in Canada, as I recollect.

At the end of the day, we had our way,

All accounted for and just one slight wreck.

The last gather ensued and final markings were made,

7-7 and C Bar C.

Branding was finished with mud to the ear,

And the fire cooled 'till next year's repeat.

In sum, a good week for us who rode mud

On the ZN that spring of '11.

We'll return in a year to the camp on the hill

And know we've returned to find Heaven.

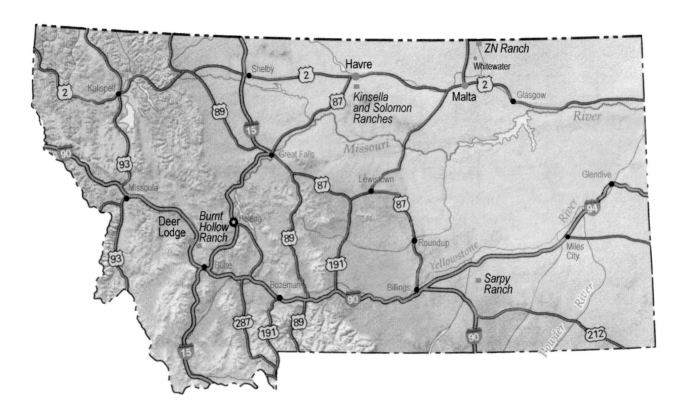

CONNIE'S MONTANA

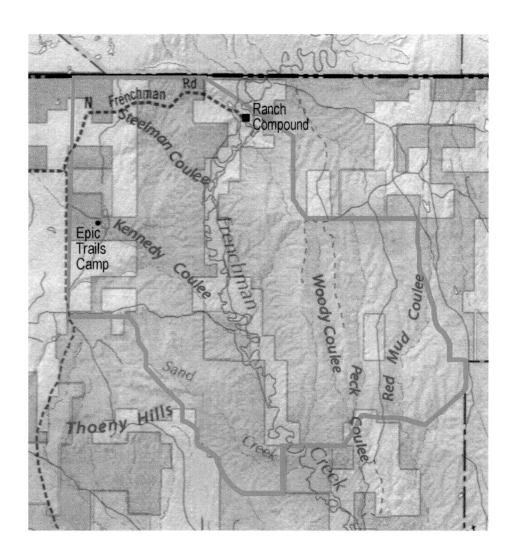

THE ZN RANCH

THE EPIC TRAILS EXPERIENCE: CONNIE COX AND HIS APPRENTICE COWBOYS

THE ENCAMPMENT

Bill Ayers

PENNY NICHOLLS

PAUL MASSON

THE RANCH COMPOUND

GATHERING CATTLE

THE APPRENTICE COWBOYS

BURNT HOLLOW RANCH NEAR DEER LODGE

KINSELLA RANCH NEAR HAVRE

. . . AND NIGHTS

THERE ARE THREE KINDS OF MEN:
THE ONE WHO LEARNS BY READING,
THE FEW WHO LEARN BY OBSERVATION,
AND THE REST OF THEM WHO HAVE
TO PEE ON THE ELECTRIC FENCE
TO FIND OUT FOR THEMSELVES.

7 • CAMPFIRE PHILOSOPHY

The first challenge for anyone new to Connie's campfire circle is deciphering the mysterious phrases that intrude into his normal conversation. You will be sitting there in the deepening dusk roasting a marshmallow over the flames. Connie will be talking about plans for the next day – where the group will ride, where to find a set of bulls, where they need to be taken – when he will veer into saying something like this:

"I cannot see. I cannot pee. I cannot chew. I cannot screw. My memory shrinks. My hearing stinks. No sense of smell. I look like hell. The golden years have come at last. The golden years can kiss my ass."

The others in the group will laugh because they have heard this a dozen times before. He will ramble on as if he had said nothing unusual, take a swig of the wine in his coffee mug and you will sit there wondering, "What just happened?"

Sometimes the errant phrase will not even be complete; something like, "When I was young and in my prime all of the girls stood in line…." You will want to say, "Yes? Go on," but this thought fragment will seem to make sense to the veteran riders around you and you will hold your tongue. Eventually, though, you will catch on to the fact that Connie's brain is crammed full of jokes, funny rhymes and bits of borrowed wisdom that spurt to the surface more erratically, but still as dependably, as the spouting waters of Old Faithful. Before long, you will have memorized many of his most well-worn lines yourself and you will know "When I was young and in my prime all of the girls stood in line" ends with "Now, I am old and gray and as I go by they look the other way."

At some point, with the smoke rising toward the first evening stars and the bottle of whiskey passing from hand to hand, someone will say, "Connie, do 'The Sky Was Dark.'" You will not know that this humorous poem of Connie's is the perennial campfire favorite and, perhaps, you will react, as Penny Nicholls did the first time she heard it, with flushed cheeks and growing alarm.

Connie will begin, "The sky was dark and the moon was high and we were alone, just her and I. Her hair was

Sally Tonkin

THE SKY WAS DARK,
THE MOON WAS HIGH
AND WE WERE ALONE,
JUST HER AND I.

HER HAIR WAS BROWN.
HER EYES WERE BLUE
AND I KNEW JUST
WHAT TO DO.

I DID IT WITH COURAGE,
I DID MY BEST,
I LAID MY HAND
UPON HER BREAST.

I TREMBLED AND SHOOK
AND FELT HER HEART
AND SLOWLY PULLED
HER FEET APART.

I KNEW SHE WAS READY
BUT I DIDN'T KNOW HOW,
FOR THIS WAS MY FIRST
OF MILKING A COW.

brown and her eyes were blue and I knew just what to do."

People around you will start grinning. Connie will continue: "I did it with courage. I did my best. I laid my hand upon her breast."

Mirthful eyes will glance your way to check your reaction.

"I trembled and shook and felt her heart – and slowly pulled her feet apart."

At this point you may be blushing, just as Penny did. And then:

"I knew she was ready. I didn't know how – for this was my first of milking a cow."

Laughter will fill the night and some of it will be at your expense because you fell for the steamy set up to this innocent tale.

Connie's jokes and storytelling are entertaining and their randomness and repetition are endearing (or, perhaps, infuriating if you are married to the man). But they are more than mere fun. They are the means he used to beat back his painful boyhood shyness and have become the way he communicates with the world. Beyond his plain wish to be an amusing companion, many of the fragments of wit and philosophy he has gathered over the years have a deeper significance. They sum up the way he looks at the world.

In shaping this book with its diverse elements, I knew I needed to first relate some of Connie's life story before delving into the maxims that are so important to him. If you understand the man, then the words gain a greater resonance. They are words he has tried to live by as best he can (though he would be the first to say he has failed as much as he has succeeded in that effort). As I culled these sayings, I saw connected threads running through them all. They are the tethers of a cowboy's life in which modesty, honesty, perseverance, loyalty and gratitude for small things are pre-eminent values.

That he is partial to cowboy poetry is no surprise. And it is certainly not surprising that one of his favorites, "The Badlands" by John D. Munn, is an elegy to his favorite part of the world. It reads, in part:

Have you ever seen the badlands?

Where the Frenchman River flows?

The mighty beef herds wander

And the diamond willow grows…

"Never judge a cowboy by what he wears. Some that look the part are not and some that don't, are." – CONNIE COX

There's something strange about their beauty

The blue haze and the tan.

It roots itself forever

In the heart of every man.

For they've shunned the brunt of ages.

Through generations, they have stood,

And a tale of many pages

They would tell you if they could

The poem goes on to recall the Indians and buffalo and Longhorns that inhabited the land and then passed into history. Then it closes:

For often in my travels,

Before the door of time does close,

I'll think of that wild country

Where the Frenchman River flows.

Poems such as this one express the sentimental feeling Connie has about his Montana home and the history he wishes he could have lived, but it is the sayings and quips that better capture his philosophy. Connie is fond of a quote from Winston Churchill: "Attitude is a little thing that makes a big difference." A right attitude is certainly what got Connie through tough experiences and primed him to seize opportunities when they came his way. It allowed him to strike out on his own at age 15. It made him game enough to climb on the back of bucking horses hundreds of times. It allowed him to make dreams a reality – a big ranch, a big cattle drive -- and then to set a new course when some dreams fell apart.

Developing a resilient attitude starts with something as obvious as using your brain:

IT'S NOT THE SIZE OF THE MAN THAT'S IN THE FIGHT,
BUT THE FIGHT THAT'S IN THE MAN THAT COUNTS.
– CONNIE COX

Competing is from the neck down, but winning is from the neck up.

In life, eight percent of the people think, 12 percent think they think and 80 percent wait for the answer.

Then, with your brain in gear, it is a matter of being smart enough to know you do not know it all. Connie likes to quote a top bronc rider from the 1950s, who said, "I hope I am wise in advice and slow to offer it, unless asked." And he matches that with a clever line from Will Rogers: "Never miss a good chance to shut up." The wisdom of thinking before you speak is born out in these observations:

Any fool can criticize, condemn, complain or lie – and most fools do.

Everybody has a knack for pointing to the problem, but very few have a knack for pointing out the solution.

In Connie's world, what is more important than telling others what to think or do is simply mastering yourself:

In life, you play the cards you're dealt, not the ones you wish you were dealt.

It's not how hard you hit, it's how hard you can get hit and keep moving forward that really makes the difference in your life.

A quitter never wins and a winner never quits.

That last observation is from the man himself. Connie has pulled together so many quotations over the years and memorized so many more that it is not always easy to know if he is quoting other people or expressing his own thoughts. Here are a few more that I am pretty sure are more or less original to him:

I would rather be all right half the time than half right all the time.

It is nice to be important, but it is more important to be nice.

Opinions are like belly buttons; we all have one of them.

One clear theme of Connie's philosophy is that we all need a good dose of humility because everyone falls short sooner or later. As he says of himself, "The best thing in life is to be honest and I have not been as honest as I should have been." At least he knows and admits it. Others have a harder time seeing their own flaws:

A clear conscience is usually the sign of a bad memory.

Going to church does not make you a Christian any more than standing in a garage makes you a car.

Yes, we are all imperfect – Connie, you, me – but that does not mean we cannot learn to recognize when it is

If you have laughter, joy and the company of a friend, you have wealth beyond silver and gold.

important to do the right thing:

Example is not the main thing in influencing others; it is the only thing.

You have to stand for what you believe in and, sometimes, you have to stand alone.

But it helps to first look at a situation from an angle other than your own:

Great Spirit, give me the power not to criticize my enemies until I have walked a mile in his moccasins.

When it comes down to it, there are just a few things that are important and essential. Near the top of Connie's list is friendship:

If you have laughter, joy and the company of a friend, you have wealth beyond silver and gold.

Or, as Helen Keller said:

Walking with a friend in the dark is better than walking alone in the light.

But as Connie has learned from riding with many men and women in harrowing circumstances where an unflinching friend made the difference between success and disaster, the finest friends are proven through experience. Or, put more elegantly by George Washington:

Be courteous to all, but intimate with few, and let those few be well tried before you give them your confidence. True friendship is a plant of slow growth and must undergo and withstand the shocks of adversity before it is entitled to the appellation.

Friends are better than enemies, after all. As world champion bull rider Lane Frost said back in 1987, "It's just as easy to make someone smile as it is to make them mad."

And so, try following this simple formula:

Live well. Laugh Often. Love much.

Connie is now at an age when love, laughter and living well are more cherished than ever. As Will Roger said, "You know you are getting old when everything either dries up or leaks." And creaks and cramps and cracks. For Connie, climbing into the saddle is not the simple boot step and swing of a leg that it once was. And climbing down from the saddle can be a precarious descent. Connie knows there is more trail behind than ahead. "I hope when I die I'll go home to Heaven," he says, "but I'm not homesick, yet."

GREAT SPIRIT, GIVE ME THE POWER NOT TO CRITICIZE MY ENEMY UNTIL I HAVE WALKED A MILE IN HIS MOCCASINS.

It has been said that humans are the only creatures that have an awareness of their own mortality. I am not sure that is entirely true. Over eons, horses have evolved with a core instinct that tells them, at any moment, they might die. Why else do their ears prick up when they sense a presence far down the path well beyond eyesight? Why else do they startle and shy when they come upon something unknown? Why else are they built to run like the wind? They know there are predators with sharp, cruel teeth that want to eat them for lunch. That knowledge makes them wary. It makes them want to stick together in a herd. It makes them prone to gallop away from anything that looks like trouble.

And, yet, if they bond with a human they trust, they will go against everything in their being that says, "flee!" They will ride into fire, cannons and churning rivers carrying a rider on their backs. They know they may die, as much as any human knows, but they are willing to die for us.

No, humans are not the only creatures with an awareness of death, but, unlike a horse, that sense of mortality causes men and women to ponder the way they live. Mark Twain said a human is the only animal that blushes – or has a reason to. Horses simply do what instinct tells them to do; humans have choices. That is why the wise ones among us seek out a philosophy, a true path, a code of conduct that might keep them from making too many bad choices and squandering the precious life they've been given.

Connie has developed his own code through a lifetime of experience and has sought out the words to express what he has come to hold true. In my estimation, all those words add up to just a few basic rules:

Whether you win or lose, just move on, stay strong and keep trying.

Admit your own flaws and enjoy laughing at yourself.

Don't preach or set yourself up as a critic; teach and lead by quiet example.

Understand that true friends are a person's greatest treasure.

Know that love and laughter create the good times and get you through the bad.

Use your mind, open your heart and do what you know is right.

Connie seems to have reached a point in life where he is weighing the way he has lived on the scale of those rules. An honest, plainspoken epitaph written by the great Montana artist Charles Russell could be Connie's own self-assessment:

Live well.
Laugh Often.
Love much.

Sally Tonkin

"IT'S JUST AS EASY TO MAKE SOMEONE SMILE AS IT IS TO MAKE THEM MAD."

— LANE FROST, WORLD CHAMPION BULL RIDER, 1987

"Over the years, I have had many friends, from rich people to poor people to preachers to sinners to cowboys. I belong to no church. I drank, but not alone. My friends were not always within the law, but I haven't said how law-abiding I am. I haven't been too good or too bad. I am a good mixer and I like most people. I was pretty wild when I was young, but age has made me gentle. There are a lot of people that are better than me, but some worse. Any man who can make a living doing what he likes is lucky and I am that. I believe in luck and have lots of it. Any time I cash in now, I win."

He ain't cashing in, yet. There are more campfires ahead for Connie, more friends to meet, more stories to tell and more lessons to impart in his very unique way to those lucky enough to sit with him by the fire or, better yet, ride out with the man on a fine, new morning.

As I said at the beginning of this book, Connie is more typical than exceptional. The things Connie knows and cares about are the things most men and women of the West know and care about if they have learned the lessons of a land that is steeped in legend, a land that is sometimes harsh and often unforgiving, but heartbreakingly beautiful and so vast that only a fool feels bigger in it than he should. Connie acknowledges he still has lessons to learn – and that may be his greatest wisdom.

Conrad Cox is not a guru, a guide, a sage or a saint. He does not belong on a pedestal. His place is in a saddle, riding on the same level as any other man, moving toward a far horizon, doing good work under storm clouds or sun and, in any circumstance, declaring with a grin, "This is livin'."

I HOPE WHEN I DIE I'LL GO HOME TO HEAVEN,
BUT I'M NOT HOMESICK, YET.
– CONNIE COX

8 • "THE SUN IS MY GOD"

Nine of us rode out with Connie Cox that bright day in late May 2011. Paul had jingled the horses at dawn while the rest of us rolled out of our tents and campers, paid our respects, one by one, to the thunder box down in the gully and tucked in a quick breakfast after saddling our horses. The air was chilly. A stiff wind whipsawed Old Glory at the top of the pole by the corral, but the sun was rising in a clear sky.

We mounted up and headed to the southeast. There were cattle to be rousted out of the rocks and thicket down by Sand Creek and off of the ridges at the southern end of the ZN Ranch. Besides Paul and Connie and me, there was Greg, a guy from Michigan who looked more like a cowboy than most cowboys. Evelyn was there, my riding partner from Los Angeles, with a smile as luminous as a Hollywood marquee. Phill, sporting chaps he had hand-tooled himself, sat astride a very fine saddle. His gung-ho cowgirl sidekick, Roxy, rode Trooper, a horse more accustomed to the wet forest trails near Seattle than the arid, open plains. Paul's girlfriend was with us – a good roper in her own right. We called her *Miss* Connie to differentiate her from our trail boss, Mr. Cox. Rounding out our crew were Steve and Betsy, an engaging couple from New York state more accustomed to polo grounds than to cowboy country.

That day I was dressed in a wheat-colored cavalry-style shirt and a red silk bandana I had picked up in Tombstone, Arizona. I had saved the outfit for the end of the week, wanting to first prove myself a decent hand, not just a dude with a snappy wardrobe. No one would mistake Connie for a dude. He was wearing his battered, black cowboy hat. A chunk of the brim was missing on the right side, a gap that looked as if a hungry horse had taken a bite. He wore the hat off kilter, putting the gap front and center.

When we came to a barbed wire gate, Connie dismounted to drag it open for the rest of us. Somebody younger should have had the good sense to do the job for him, but, on this morning, Connie was in high spirits, feeling good and riding like a much younger man. As he hauled himself back into the saddle he tossed off a joke that got carried away in the wind before I could hear it. I laughed anyway. After all, I had probably heard it before.

We were riding across a rolling expanse of short grass. Weeks of torrential rains had swollen Montana's rivers, flooded half the state and turned the rodeo grounds at the Bucking Horse Sale in Miles City into a sea of mud. Up here near the border, though, the main effect of the wet spring was to paint the countryside a lush green. Wild flowers

THE SUN IS MY GOD,
THE OUTSIDE IS MY CHURCH,
NATURE IS MY SCHOOL ROOM
AND I KNOW ALL OF ITS PAGES.

were scattered across the prairie like a million yellow stars in a green sky.

Greg rode far off to the side much of the time. He preferred a lope across the hills to the steady walk of the main troop. He had not traveled all the way from Michigan to be confined to a slow pace. Phill pulled out his harmonica and played a tune. Few would guess that back in Seattle he worked as an investment banker. Roxy was liberated. For once, she was not stealing riding time in between her young sons' school and sports activities. Out here this week she could ride, ride, ride. Evelyn was quietly drinking it all in, feeling profoundly lucky to be in this place on this day instead of fielding phone calls from clients back in LA.

All of us were feeling free. We came from different places and different walks of life, but we shared the same romantic notion that there were few finer endeavors in the world than riding on the back of a horse in the Great American West.

Our small troop rode on for a half hour until the gentle rise and fall of the prairie abruptly stopped at a cliff's edge. We reined our horses and quietly drank in the scene. Down rough coulees and steep breaks, the earth fell away into a broad valley of dramatic badlands. The pastel shades of sandy ground, gray rock, tanned hillocks, pale green sage and deeper green grass formed a crazy quilt pattern on the twisted land. Behind a distant hill, the serpentine course of Frenchman Creek wound down from Canada. Far beyond that, another ridge rose up where the prairie began again and the ZN Ranch finally came to an end.

Connie shifted in his saddle and joked about a friend he had brought to this place. He told the friend this was the top of the world, "as close to Heaven as you'll ever get," and the friend said that was fine, none of his pals would be up there anyway.

It was obvious this place was close to Heaven for Connie. It was the beckoning ranchland he had spotted from an airplane on the way back from a rodeo, the place he had scouted on horseback before moving his young family to grow up here and learn cowboy ways. This land had changed very little since the days long gone when the Indians called it home, he said – "No airplanes, no cars, no fast motorcycles." He lifted his arms and began to recite an old Indian saying:

"The sun is my god, the outside is my church, nature is my schoolroom and I know all of its pages."

Connie glanced at each of us. "You think about that," he said. "That was the Indians. Just take this in. Take a look at it." And take it in we did – not just the rugged beauty that stretched out below, but the words of the Indians and, most of all, the good man who had just spoken them.

Then, we descended into the valley and got to work.

AUTHOR AND PHOTOGRAPHER

Two-time Pulitzer Prize-winning journalist DAVID HORSEY is a political cartoonist and columnist
for the Los Angeles Times. Among his many honors, he took first place in the Best of the West
Journalism Competition for a series of columns about the 2008 presidential campaign in the western states.
His greatest accomplishment is raising two fine children, his daughter, Darielle, and son, Daniel.
David lives in Seattle with the girl he fell in love with in high school -- his wife, Nole Ann.
Whenever he can steal a week or two, David runs off to Montana to work as an apprentice cowboy.

ADDITIONAL PHOTOGRAPHY

SALLY TONKIN, a former newspaper photographer, is now a photography teacher in Yakima, Washington. She earned an MFA at the University of Washington. The daughter of an Ellensburg Rodeo princess, Sally was a competitive rider in her younger days.

BILL AYERS is a glass artist who teaches the craft in Redmond, Washington. Bill has made frequent trips to the ZN, not only to ride and move cattle, but to take on some of the tougher ranch jobs, from digging post holes to mucking out stalls.

EPIC TRAILS – ENDLESS TRACKS ACROSS CENTURIES
By Conrad "Connie" Cox and Dr. Jim Scott
With photography by Cal Sorenson

The only complete account of The Great Montana Centennial Cattle Drive of 1989 is now available at reduced prices in three formats:

• **Limited edition collector's volume, case bound in bonded leather, signed and numbered -- $75**
• **Hardbound book, simulated leather cover -- $35**
• **Soft cover book -- $15**

All books are 8.5"x11" and 256 pages.

To purchase this unique volume about a grand once-in-a-century adventure, send your mailing address and phone number with payment for each book ordered, plus $3.00 shipping for each item, to:

Conrad Cox
49546 Eagle Rock Road
Havre, MT 59501

For more information, call: (406) 395-5336

Made in the USA
Charleston, SC
14 February 2013